HOW TO WAKE UP RICHER EVERY DAY

The Secrets of Making Money While You Sleep

Luis W. Ralph

Please consider writing a review!

Copyright © 2023 Luis W. Ralph

TABLE OF CONTENTS

INTRODUCTION

Why You Need to Make Money While You Sleep

Have you ever dreamed of waking up richer every day? Imagine how amazing it would be to check your bank account in the morning and see that you have earned more money while you were sleeping than most people do in a month. Sounds too good to be true, right?

Well, it's not. In fact, it's possible for anyone who is willing to learn the secrets of making money while you sleep. And in this book, I'm going to share with you the exact strategies and techniques that I have used to create multiple streams of passive income that generate thousands of dollars every month, even when I'm not working.

But before we dive into the details, let me tell you a little bit about myself and why I decided to write this book.

My name is Luis W. Ralph, and I'm a self-made millionaire. I wasn't born into a wealthy family, nor did I inherit a fortune from a distant relative. I grew up in a modest home in Lisbon, Portugal, where my parents worked hard to provide for me and my siblings. They taught me the value of education, hard work, and honesty.

I followed their advice and studied hard in school. I graduated from the University of Lisbon with a degree in computer science and landed a job as a software engineer at a reputable company. I was earning a decent salary, but I was also spending long hours in front of a computer, dealing with deadlines, stress, and office politics. I felt like I was trading my time for money, and I wasn't happy.

I wanted more out of life. I wanted to have more freedom, more flexibility, and more fun. I wanted to travel the world, pursue my passions, and make a positive impact on others. I wanted to live life on my own terms.

That's when I discovered the power of passive income. Passive income is money that you earn without actively working for it. It's money that comes to you automatically, whether you are awake or asleep, whether you are at home or on vacation, whether you are working or not.

There are many ways to create passive income, such as investing in stocks, bonds, real estate, or cryptocurrencies; creating digital products like ebooks, courses, or software; or building online businesses like blogs, podcasts, or ecommerce stores.

I decided to try them all. I read books, watched videos, listened to podcasts, and attended seminars on how to make money online. I learned from the best experts and mentors in the field. I experimented with different ideas and methods. I failed many times, but I also succeeded many times. Over the years, I have built multiple streams of passive income that generate over $100,000 per month for me. And the best part is that I don't have to work for it anymore. It's all automated and systematized. It runs on autopilot.

This has allowed me to achieve financial freedom and live the life of my dreams. I have traveled to over 50 countries around the world. I have met amazing people and experienced different cultures. I have pursued my hobbies and interests without worrying about money. I have donated to various causes and charities that are close to my heart. I have enjoyed every moment of my life.

And now, I want to help you do the same. That's why I wrote this book, How to Wake Up Richer Every Day: The Secrets of Making Money While You Sleep.

In this book, you will learn:

- The benefits of passive income and why it's the key to financial freedom
- The mindset and habits that you need to develop to succeed in making money while you sleep
- The best passive income ideas and opportunities that you can start today
- The step-by-step process of creating your own passive income streams from scratch
- The tools and resources that you need to automate and scale your passive income business
- The tips and tricks that will help you avoid common mistakes and pitfalls
- The case studies and examples of real people who have achieved amazing results with passive income
- And much more!

By the end of this book, you will have everything you need to start making money while you sleep. You will be able to create multiple sources of income that will grow over time and provide you with consistent cash flow. You will be able to achieve financial independence and live the life that you deserve.

Are you ready to wake up richer every day?If so, then let's get started!

CHAPTER
1

The Mindset of a Passive Income Earner

What if you could wake up richer every day without having to work hard for it? What if you could make money while you sleep, travel, or enjoy your hobbies? What if you could achieve financial freedom and live the life of your dreams?

Sounds too good to be true, right? Well, it's not. It's possible, and it's called passive income.

Passive income is money that you earn without active involvement or effort. It's money that works for you, instead of you working for money. It's money that grows on its own, without requiring your constant attention or supervision. It's money that gives you more time, more freedom, and more happiness.

But how do you create passive income? How do you find the right opportunities, the right strategies, and the right systems to generate consistent and reliable income streams that can support your lifestyle and goals?

The answer is simple: you need to have the mindset of a passive income earner.

The mindset of a passive income earner is the key to unlocking the secrets of making money while you sleep. It's the way of thinking, feeling, and acting that enables you to identify, create, and leverage passive income sources that suit your skills, interests, and passions. It's the attitude, the belief, and the vision that empowers you to overcome the challenges, the risks, and the uncertainties that come with building wealth and achieving success.

In this chapter, we will explore the essential elements of the mindset of a passive income earner. We will learn how to:

- Shift from a scarcity mindset to an abundance mindset
- Adopt a growth mindset instead of a fixed mindset
- Develop a long-term perspective rather than a short-term focus
- Embrace creativity and innovation over conformity and imitation
- Cultivate curiosity and learning over complacency and stagnation
- Foster resilience and perseverance over fear and doubt
- Seek value creation and problem solving over profit chasing and competition

- Build systems and automation over dependence and micromanagement
- Leverage other people's time, money, and expertise over self-reliance and isolation
- Enjoy the journey and celebrate the milestones over stressing over the destination and the outcome

By mastering these aspects of the mindset of a passive income earner, you will be able to unlock your full potential and achieve your financial goals faster and easier than ever before. You will be able to create multiple streams of income that will provide you with passive cash flow, passive appreciation, passive tax benefits, passive diversification, and passive protection. You will be able to wake up richer every day and live the life of your dreams.

Shift from a scarcity mindset to an abundance mindset

One of the most important elements of the mindset of a passive income earner is to shift from a scarcity mindset to an abundance mindset. A scarcity mindset is the belief that there is not enough for everyone, that resources are limited, and that you have to compete and struggle to get what you want. A scarcity mindset leads to fear, anxiety, stress, and resentment. It makes you focus on what you lack, what you can lose, and what you can't have. It makes you settle for less, compromise your values, and sacrifice your happiness.

An abundance mindset is the belief that there is more than enough for everyone, that resources are plentiful, and that you can cooperate and collaborate to get what you want. An abundance mindset leads to confidence, optimism, gratitude, and generosity. It makes you focus on what you have, what you can gain, and what you can create. It makes you strive for more, align with your purpose, and pursue your passion.

To shift from a scarcity mindset to an abundance mindset, you need to:

- Challenge your limiting beliefs and assumptions about money, wealth, and success. Replace them with empowering beliefs and affirmations that support your goals and vision.
- Practice gratitude and appreciation for what you have and what you receive. Express your gratitude to yourself, to others, and to the universe.
- Adopt a positive attitude and outlook on life. Focus on the opportunities, the possibilities, and the solutions rather than the problems, the obstacles, and the challenges.

- Share your knowledge, skills, and resources with others. Help others succeed and grow. Give value without expecting anything in return.
- Seek abundance in all areas of your life. Not just money, but also health, relationships, happiness, and fulfillment.

By shifting from a scarcity mindset to an abundance mindset, you will be able to attract more wealth and abundance into your life. You will be able to create passive income sources that align with your values and passions. You will be able to wake up richer every day in every way.

Adopt a growth mindset instead of a fixed mindset

Another essential element of the mindset of a passive income earner is to adopt a growth mindset instead of a fixed mindset. A fixed mindset is the belief that your abilities, talents, and intelligence are fixed and cannot be changed. A fixed mindset leads to complacency, stagnation, and resistance to change. It makes you avoid challenges, give up easily, ignore feedback, and feel threatened by the success of others. It makes you believe that you are either good or bad at something, and that there is nothing you can do to improve.

A growth mindset is the belief that your abilities, talents, and intelligence can be developed and improved through effort, learning, and practice. A growth mindset leads to curiosity, innovation, and adaptation. It makes you embrace challenges, persist in the face of setbacks, seek feedback, and celebrate the success of others. It makes you believe that you can always learn something new, grow from your mistakes, and achieve your potential.

To adopt a growth mindset instead of a fixed mindset, you need to:

- Recognize your fixed mindset triggers and thoughts. Identify the situations and emotions that make you feel insecure, defensive, or discouraged. Challenge the negative thoughts and beliefs that hold you back.
- Replace your fixed mindset statements with growth mindset statements. For example, instead of saying "I can't do this", say "I can learn how to do this". Instead of saying "This is too hard", say "This is an opportunity to grow". Instead of saying "I'm not good enough", say "I can improve with practice".
- Set realistic and specific goals for yourself. Break down your big goals into smaller and manageable steps. Track your progress and celebrate your achievements.
- Seek feedback and learn from it. Ask for constructive criticism and advice from others who have more experience or expertise

than you. Listen to their suggestions and apply them to your work.

- Learn from your failures and mistakes. Don't let them define you or discourage you. Analyze what went wrong and what you can do better next time. Treat them as learning opportunities and not as personal flaws.

By adopting a growth mindset instead of a fixed mindset, you will be able to enhance your skills, knowledge, and performance. You will be able to create passive income sources that challenge you, inspire you, and reward you. You will be able to wake up richer every day in every way.

Develop a long-term perspective rather than a short-term focus

Another crucial element of the mindset of a passive income earner is to develop a long-term perspective rather than a short-term focus. A short-term focus is the tendency to prioritize immediate gratification, quick results, and instant rewards. A short-term focus leads to impatience, frustration, and distraction. It makes you chase shiny objects, jump from one thing to another, and lose sight of your vision. It makes you sacrifice your future for your present, and compromise your quality for your quantity.

A long-term perspective is the ability to plan ahead, delay gratification, and invest in your future. A long-term perspective leads to patience, persistence, and discipline. It makes you stick to your goals, follow your strategies, and align with your vision. It makes you build your future for your present, and enhance your quality for your quantity.

To develop a long-term perspective rather than a short-term focus, you need to:

- Define your vision and purpose. What do you want to achieve in your life? Why do you want to achieve it? How will it make you feel? Write down your vision and purpose in a clear and compelling way.
- Set SMART goals for yourself. SMART stands for Specific, Measurable, Achievable, Relevant, and Time-bound. Make sure your goals are aligned with your vision and purpose, and that they are realistic and attainable.
- Break down your goals into action steps. What do you need to do to achieve your goals? What are the tasks, activities, and actions that will move you closer to your desired outcome? Create a plan and a schedule for each step.
- Track your progress and measure your results. How do you know if you are on the right track? How do you know if you

are getting closer to your goals? Use tools and methods to monitor and evaluate your performance and outcomes.

- Reward yourself for your achievements. How do you celebrate your successes? How do you acknowledge your efforts and accomplishments? Give yourself incentives and rewards for reaching your milestones and completing your tasks.

By developing a long-term perspective rather than a short-term focus, you will be able to create passive income sources that last, grow, and multiply over time. You will be able to wake up richer every day in every way.

Embrace creativity and innovation over conformity and imitation

Another vital element of the mindset of a passive income earner is to embrace creativity and innovation over conformity and imitation. Conformity and imitation are the tendencies to follow the crowd, copy the trends, and do what everyone else is doing. Conformity and imitation lead to mediocrity, saturation, and competition. They make you lose your uniqueness, your edge, and your value. They make you blend in, rather than stand out.

Creativity and innovation are the abilities to think outside the box, create something new, and do what no one else is doing. Creativity and innovation lead to excellence, differentiation, and collaboration. They make you express your uniqueness, your edge, and your value. They make you stand out, rather than blend in.

To embrace creativity and innovation over conformity and imitation, you need to:

- Find your niche and passion. What are you good at? What do you enjoy doing? What problems can you solve? What value can you provide? Identify your niche and passion that match your skills, interests, and goals.

- Research your market and audience. Who are your potential customers? What are their needs, wants, and desires? What are their pain points, challenges, and frustrations? What are their goals, dreams, and aspirations? Understand your market and audience that can benefit from your niche and passion.

- Develop your unique selling proposition (USP). What makes you different from others in your niche? What makes you better than others in your niche? What makes you the best choice for your customers? Craft your USP that showcases your uniqueness, your edge, and your value.

- Create your minimum viable product (MVP). What is the simplest version of your product or service that can deliver your USP to your customers? What are the essential features and benefits that your product or service must have? How can you test and validate your product or service with real customers? Build your MVP that demonstrates your creativity, your innovation, and your solution.

- Iterate and improve your product or service. How can you get feedback from your customers? How can you measure the performance and results of your product or service? How can you enhance the quality and value of your product or service? How can you scale up and expand your product or service? Refine your product or service that reflects your learning, your growth, and your improvement.

By embracing creativity and innovation over conformity and imitation, you will be able to create passive income sources that are unique, valuable, and profitable. You will be able to wake up richer every day in every way.

Cultivate curiosity and learning over complacency and stagnation

Another important element of the mindset of a passive income earner is to cultivate curiosity and learning over complacency and stagnation. Complacency and stagnation are the states of being satisfied with the status quo, unwilling to change, and resistant to growth. Complacency and stagnation lead to boredom, decay, and obsolescence. They make you miss out on new opportunities, new trends, and new developments. They make you fall behind, rather than stay ahead.

Curiosity and learning are the states of being interested in the unknown, eager to change, and open to growth. Curiosity and learning lead to excitement, improvement, and relevance. They make you discover new opportunities, new trends, and new developments. They make you stay ahead, rather than fall behind.

To cultivate curiosity and learning over complacency and stagnation, you need to:

- Adopt a beginner's mind. What if you knew nothing about your niche, your market, or your product? What if you had to start from scratch? How would you approach it differently? What questions would you ask? What assumptions would you challenge? What experiments would you conduct? Approach your niche, your market, or your product with a beginner's mind that is curious, humble, and flexible.

- Read books and articles. What are the best books and articles on your niche, your market, or your product? What are the latest books and articles on your niche, your market, or your product? What are the most recommended books and articles on your niche, your market, or your product? Read books and articles that can expand your knowledge, update your information, and inspire your ideas.

- Watch videos and podcasts. What are the best videos and podcasts on your niche, your market, or your product? What are the latest videos and podcasts on your niche, your market, or your product? What are the most popular videos and podcasts on your niche, your market, or your product? Watch videos and podcasts that can enhance your skills, showcase your examples, and motivate your actions.

- Take courses and workshops. What are the best courses and workshops on your niche, your market, or your product? What are the latest courses and workshops on your niche, your market, or your product? What are the most relevant courses and workshops on your niche, your market, or your product? Take courses and workshops that can teach you new concepts, new methods, and new strategies.

- Join communities and networks. What are the best communities and networks on your niche, your market, or your product? What are the latest communities and networks on your niche, your market, or your product? What are the most active communities and networks on your niche, your market, or your product? Join communities and networks that can connect you with other people who share your interests, goals, and passions.

By cultivating curiosity and learning over complacency and stagnation, you will be able to create passive income sources that are fresh, innovative, and valuable. You will be able to wake up richer every day in every way.

Foster resilience and perseverance over fear and doubt

Another key element of the mindset of a passive income earner is to foster resilience and perseverance over fear and doubt. Fear and doubt are the emotions that make you hesitate, procrastinate, and give up on your goals. Fear and doubt lead to insecurity, anxiety, and stress. They make you avoid risks, reject opportunities, and sabotage your success. They make you think of the worst-case scenarios, rather than the best-case scenarios.

Resilience and perseverance are the qualities that make you overcome obstacles, cope with challenges, and persist in your goals. Resilience and perseverance lead to confidence, courage, and determination. They make you take risks, seize opportunities, and achieve your success. They make you think of the best-case scenarios, rather than the worst-case scenarios.

To foster resilience and perseverance over fear and doubt, you need to:

- Identify your fears and doubts. What are you afraid of? What are you doubtful about? What are the sources and causes of your fears and doubts? How do they affect your thoughts, feelings, and actions? Acknowledge your fears and doubts without judging or denying them.

- Challenge your fears and doubts. Are your fears and doubts rational or irrational? Are they based on facts or assumptions? Are they helpful or harmful? How likely are they to happen? How can you prevent or cope with them? Challenge your fears and doubts with logic, evidence, and positive thinking.

- Face your fears and doubts. What can you do to confront your fears and doubts? What can you do to overcome them? What can you do to learn from them? How can you use them as motivation and inspiration? Face your fears and doubts with action, experimentation, and feedback.

- Build your resilience and perseverance. What can you do to strengthen your resilience and perseverance? What can you do to boost your self-esteem, self-efficacy, and self-compassion? What can you do to develop your coping skills, problem-solving skills, and goal-setting skills? How can you use your support network, mentors, and role models? Build your resilience and perseverance with practice, learning, and growth.

By fostering resilience and perseverance over fear and doubt, you will be able to create passive income sources that are challenging, rewarding, and fulfilling. You will be able to wake up richer every day in every way.

Seek value creation and problem solving over profit chasing and competition

Another essential element of the mindset of a passive income earner is to seek value creation and problem solving over profit chasing and competition. Profit chasing and competition are the motivations that make you focus on making money, beating others, and winning at all costs. Profit chasing and competition lead to greed, envy, and stress. They make you ignore your customers, your values, and your purpose. They make you chase money, rather than money chase you.

Value creation and problem solving are the motivations that make you focus on providing value, helping others, and making a difference. Value creation and problem solving lead to generosity, satisfaction, and fulfillment. They make you serve your customers, your values, and your purpose. They make money chase you, rather than you chase money.

To seek value creation and problem solving over profit chasing and competition, you need to:

- Identify your customers' problems and needs. What are the biggest problems and needs that your customers have? What are the most urgent, important, and common problems and needs that your customers have? How do they affect their lives, their goals, and their happiness? Understand your customers' problems and needs from their perspective.

- Create value propositions for your customers. What are the best solutions and benefits that you can offer to your customers? What are the unique advantages and features that you can offer to your customers? How do they solve their problems, meet their needs, and improve their lives? Craft value propositions that communicate your value creation and problem solving to your customers.

- Deliver value to your customers. How can you deliver your value propositions to your customers in the most effective and efficient way? How can you ensure the quality, reliability, and consistency of your value delivery? How can you exceed your customers' expectations and delight them? Implement value delivery systems that deliver your value creation and problem solving to your customers.

- Get feedback from your customers. How can you get feedback from your customers on your value propositions and value delivery? How can you measure the satisfaction, loyalty, and referrals of your customers? How can you use feedback to improve your value propositions and value delivery? Collect feedback from your customers that reflects your value creation and problem solving for your customers.

- Repeat the process. How can you create more value and solve more problems for your customers? How can you find new customers or new markets for your value propositions? How can you leverage your existing customers or existing markets for your value propositions? Repeat the process of value creation and problem solving for your customers.

By seeking value creation and problem solving over profit chasing and competition, you will be able to create passive income sources that are meaningful, impactful, and sustainable. You will be able to wake up richer every day in every way.

Build systems and automation over dependence and micromanagement

Another important element of the mindset of a passive income earner is to build systems and automation over dependence and micromanagement. Dependence and micromanagement are the habits of relying on others or yourself to do everything, controlling every detail, and being involved in every process. Dependence and micromanagement lead to stress, burnout, and inefficiency. They make you waste your time, energy, and money on tasks that are not essential, not scalable, or not enjoyable. They make you work in your business, rather than on your business.

Systems and automation are the methods of creating processes, procedures, and tools that can run your business without your constant intervention or supervision. Systems and automation lead to freedom, productivity, and profitability. They make you save your time, energy, and money on tasks that are essential, scalable, and enjoyable. They make you work on your business, rather than in your business.

To build systems and automation over dependence and micromanagement, you need to:

- Document your business processes. What are the steps, actions, and decisions that you take to run your business? What are the inputs, outputs, and outcomes of each process? What are the roles, responsibilities, and resources involved in each process? Write down your business processes in a clear and detailed way.
- Optimize your business processes. How can you improve your business processes to make them more effective and efficient? How can you eliminate, simplify, or combine steps, actions, or

decisions? How can you reduce errors, risks, or costs? How can you increase quality, speed, or value? Refine your business processes to make them more optimal and streamlined.

- Automate your business processes. How can you use technology, software, or tools to automate your business processes? How can you use artificial intelligence, machine learning, or data analytics to automate your business processes? How can you use outsourcing, delegation, or collaboration to automate your business processes? Implement automation solutions that can run your business processes without your involvement or supervision.

- Monitor and evaluate your business processes. How can you track and measure the performance and results of your business processes? How can you get feedback and data on your business processes? How can you use key performance indicators (KPIs), dashboards, or reports to monitor and evaluate your business processes? Use monitoring and evaluation tools that can provide you with insights and information on your business processes.

- Update and improve your business processes. How can you keep your business processes up to date and relevant? How can you adapt your business processes to changing market conditions, customer preferences, or industry standards? How can you enhance your business processes to create more value, solve more problems, or generate more income? Update and improve your business processes based on your learning and growth.

By building systems and automation over dependence and micromanagement, you will be able to create passive income sources that are scalable, reliable, and consistent. You will be able to wake up richer every day in every way.

Leverage other people's time, money, and expertise over self-reliance and isolation

Another essential element of the mindset of a passive income earner is to leverage other people's time, money, and expertise over self-reliance and isolation. Self-reliance and isolation are the tendencies to do everything by yourself, rely on your own resources, and avoid working with others. Self-reliance and isolation lead to exhaustion, limitation, and missed opportunities. They make you work harder, not smarter. They make you limit your potential, rather than expand your possibilities.

Leverage is the ability to use other people's time, money, and expertise to achieve more with less. Leverage is the power to multiply your results, increase your resources, and access new opportunities. Leverage is the skill to work smarter, not harder. Leverage is the strategy to expand your possibilities, rather than limit your potential.

To leverage other people's time, money, and expertise over self-reliance and isolation, you need to:

- Build your team. Who are the people that can help you run your business? Who are the people that can complement your skills, fill your gaps, and share your vision? How can you find, hire, train, and manage them? Create a team that can support you, assist you, and collaborate with you.

- Raise your capital. How much money do you need to start or grow your business? How can you get funding from investors, lenders, or partners? How can you use crowdfunding, grants, or donations? How can you manage your cash flow, budget, and expenses? Secure capital that can finance you, invest in you, and partner with you.

- Learn from your mentors. Who are the experts in your niche, market, or industry? Who are the successful passive income earners that you admire or aspire to be? How can you connect with them, learn from them, and get advice from them? Find mentors that can guide you, teach you, and inspire you.

By leveraging other people's time, money, and expertise over self-reliance and isolation, you will be able to create passive income sources that are faster, easier, and better. You will be able to wake up richer every day in every way.

Enjoy the journey and celebrate the milestones over stressing over the destination and the outcome

The last but not the least element of the mindset of a passive income earner is to enjoy the journey and celebrate the milestones over stressing over the destination and the outcome. Stressing over the destination and the outcome is the habit of focusing on the end result, the final goal, and the ultimate reward. Stressing over the destination and the outcome leads to pressure, anxiety, and disappointment. It makes you miss the present moment, the learning process, and the small wins. It makes you attach your happiness to your success, rather than your success to your happiness.

Enjoying the journey and celebrating the milestones is the habit of focusing on the present moment, the learning process, and the small wins. Enjoying the journey and celebrating the milestones leads to joy, gratitude, and fulfillment. It makes you appreciate the present moment, the learning process, and the small wins. It makes you attach your success to your happiness, rather than your happiness to your success.

To enjoy the journey and celebrate the milestones over stressing over the destination and the outcome, you need to:

- Be mindful and present. How can you be more aware of your thoughts, feelings, and actions? How can you be more attentive to your surroundings, your environment, and your situation? How can you be more engaged in your activities, your tasks, and your goals? Practice mindfulness and presence that can help you enjoy the journey.

- Be grateful and appreciative. What are you grateful for in your life? What are you appreciative of in your business? What are you thankful for in your customers? Express gratitude and appreciation that can help you enjoy the journey.

- Be playful and fun. How can you make your work more fun and enjoyable? How can you inject humor, creativity, and excitement into your work? How can you balance your work with your hobbies, interests, and passions? Have fun and play that can help you enjoy the journey.

- Set milestones and rewards. What are the sub-goals that lead to your main goal? What are the indicators that show your progress and achievements? What are the incentives and rewards that motivate and inspire you? Create milestones and rewards that can help you celebrate the milestones.

- Share your stories and successes. Who are the people that support you, encourage you, and celebrate with you? How can you share your stories, experiences, and lessons with them? How can you share your successes, achievements, and results with them? Connect with others that can help you celebrate the milestones.

By enjoying the journey and celebrating the milestones over stressing over the destination and the outcome, you will be able to create passive income sources that are not only profitable, but also enjoyable. You will be able to wake up richer every day in every way.

This concludes chapter 1 of "How to Wake Up Richer Every Day: The Secrets of Making Money While You Sleep". I hope you found it helpful and informative. In chapter 2, we will explore some of the best passive income ideas that you can start today. Stay tuned!

CHAPTER
2

The Best Passive Income Streams for 2023 and Beyond

In the previous chapter, we learned about the mindset of a passive income earner, and how to develop the essential elements that can help you create and leverage passive income sources. In this chapter, we will explore some of the best passive income ideas that you can start today, and how to choose the ones that suit your skills, interests, and goals.

Passive income is money that you earn without active involvement or effort. It's money that works for you, instead of you working for money. It's money that grows on its own, without requiring your constant attention or supervision. It's money that gives you more time, more freedom, and more happiness.

But how do you create passive income? How do you find the right opportunities, the right strategies, and the right systems to generate consistent and reliable income streams that can support your lifestyle and goals?

The answer is simple: you need to have a portfolio of passive income streams.

A portfolio of passive income streams is a collection of different sources of income that can complement each other, diversify your risk, and maximize your potential. A portfolio of passive income streams can help you achieve financial freedom and live the life of your dreams.

But what are the best passive income streams for 2023 and beyond? What are the most profitable, scalable, and sustainable passive income sources that you can start today?

There are many passive income ideas out there, but not all of them are created equal. Some of them may require a lot of upfront investment, time, or skills. Some of them may be too competitive, too risky, or too volatile. Some of them may be outdated, irrelevant, or obsolete.

To help you choose the best passive income streams for 2023 and beyond, we have compiled a list of 10 passive income ideas that are:

- Proven and tested by successful passive income earners

- Easy and affordable to start with minimal investment, time, or skills
- Flexible and adaptable to changing market conditions, customer preferences, or industry standards
- Scalable and profitable to generate high returns, low costs, and high margins
- Sustainable and consistent to provide long-term value, growth, and stability

These 10 passive income ideas are:
- Affiliate Marketing
- Blogging
- Podcasting
- YouTube
- Online Courses
- E-books
- Software as a Service (SaaS)
- Mobile Apps
- E-commerce
- Dropshipping

Let's take a closer look at each of these passive income ideas, and see how they work, how to start them, and how to succeed with them.

Affiliate Marketing

Affiliate marketing is one of the most popular and lucrative passive income ideas. Affiliate marketing is the process of promoting other people's products or services and earning a commission for every sale or action that you generate. Affiliate marketing is a win-win situation for both the product owner and the affiliate marketer. The product owner gets more exposure, traffic, and sales for their product or service. The affiliate marketer gets a percentage of the revenue without having to create or deliver the product or service.

How does affiliate marketing work?

Affiliate marketing works in four simple steps:

1. You join an affiliate program or network that offers products or services that are relevant to your niche, market, or audience.

2. You get an affiliate link or code that tracks your referrals and commissions.

3. You promote the affiliate product or service to your audience through your website, blog, social media, email list, podcast, YouTube channel, or any other platform.

4. You earn a commission every time someone clicks on your affiliate link or code and buys the product or service.

How do you start affiliate marketing?

To start affiliate marketing, you need to:

1. Choose a niche that you are interested in, passionate about, or knowledgeable about.

2. Research the best affiliate programs or networks that offer products or services in your niche.

3. Sign up for the affiliate programs or networks that suit your goals and preferences.

4. Create valuable content that attracts your target audience and provides solutions to their problems or needs.

5. Add your affiliate links or codes to your content in a natural and ethical way.

6. Drive traffic to your content through SEO (search engine optimization), social media marketing, email marketing, paid advertising, or any other method.

7. Track and optimize your performance and results using analytics tools and reports.

How do you succeed with affiliate marketing?

To succeed with affiliate marketing, you need to:

1. Choose high-quality products or services that provide value to your audience and solve their problems or needs.

2. Choose reputable affiliate programs or networks that offer fair commissions, timely payments, and good support.

3. Build trust and credibility with your audience by providing honest reviews, testimonials, case studies, or comparisons of the products or services that you promote.

4. Provide bonuses, incentives, discounts, or freebies to entice your audience to buy through your affiliate links or codes.

5. Test and experiment with different products, services, offers, headlines, images, videos, or calls to action to see what works best for your audience and conversions.

6. Follow the rules and regulations of the affiliate programs or networks that you join, and avoid spamming, misleading, or violating the terms and conditions.

7. Keep learning and improving your skills, knowledge, and strategies by following the best practices, tips, and trends in affiliate marketing.

Affiliate marketing is one of the best passive income streams for 2023 and beyond because it is:

- Proven and tested by successful passive income earners who make thousands or millions of dollars per month from affiliate marketing.

- Easy and affordable to start with minimal investment, time, or skills. You don't need to create or deliver the product or service. You just need to promote it to your audience.

- Flexible and adaptable to changing market conditions, customer preferences, or industry standards. You can choose from a wide range of products or services in any niche or market. You can also switch or add products or services as you wish.
- Scalable and profitable to generate high returns, low costs, and high margins. You can earn passive income from multiple sources, multiple platforms, and multiple audiences. You can also earn recurring commissions from subscription-based products or services.
- Sustainable and consistent to provide long-term value, growth, and stability. You can build a loyal and engaged audience that trusts you and buys from you repeatedly. You can also leverage the power of SEO (search engine optimization), social media marketing, email marketing, paid advertising, or any other method to drive traffic to your content.

If you want to learn more about affiliate marketing, you can check out these resources:

- The Ultimate Guide to Affiliate Marketing by Pat Flynn
- Affiliate Marketing for Beginners: 7 Steps to Success by Adam Enfroy
- Affiliate Marketing Made Simple: A Step-by-Step Guide by Neil Patel

Blogging

Blogging is another popular and lucrative passive income idea. Blogging is the process of creating and publishing content on a website or platform that covers a specific topic or niche. Blogging is a great way to share your knowledge, passion, or expertise with your audience. Blogging is also a great way to generate passive income from various sources such as advertising, sponsored posts, affiliate marketing, online courses, e-books, software as a service (SaaS), mobile apps, e-commerce, dropshipping, or any other method.

How does blogging work?

Blogging works in four simple steps:

1. You choose a niche that you are interested in, passionate about, or knowledgeable about.

2. You create a website or platform where you can publish your content.

3. You write valuable content that attracts your target audience and provides solutions to their problems or needs.

4. You monetize your content with various methods that suit your goals and preferences.

How do you start blogging?

To start blogging, you need to:

1. Choose a niche that has a large and engaged audience, high demand and low competition, and profitable monetization potential.

2. Choose a domain name that is catchy, memorable, and relevant to your niche.

3. Choose a web hosting service that is reliable, fast, and affordable.

4. Choose a blogging platform that is easy to use, flexible, and customizable. WordPress is the most popular and recommended blogging platform.

5. Choose a theme that is attractive, responsive, and functional for your website or platform.

6. Choose plugins that can enhance the features and performance of your website or platform.

7. Create valuable content that attracts your target audience and provides solutions to their problems or needs. Use keywords, headlines, images, videos, links, or any other elements that can optimize your content for SEO (search engine optimization) and user experience.

8. Drive traffic to your content through SEO (search engine optimization), social media marketing, email marketing, paid advertising, or any other method.

How do you succeed with blogging?

To succeed with blogging, you need to:

1. Choose a niche that you are interested in, passionate about, or knowledgeable about. This will help you create content that is authentic, engaging, and consistent.

2. Choose a domain name that is catchy, memorable, and relevant to your niche. This will help you build your brand identity and recognition.

3. Choose a web hosting service that is reliable, fast, and affordable. This will help you ensure the security and performance of your website or platform.

4. Choose a blogging platform that is easy to use, flexible, and customizable. WordPress is the most popular and recommended blogging platform because it offers thousands of themes and plugins that can suit any niche or need.

5. Choose a theme that is attractive responsive ,and functional for your website or platform. This will help you create a professional-looking website or platform that can attract and retain your visitors.

6. Choose plugins that can enhance the features and performance of your website or platform. This will help you add functionality and performance to your website or platform that can improve your user experience and conversions.

7. Create valuable content that attracts your target audience and provides solutions to their problems or needs. This will help you

establish your authority, credibility, and trustworthiness in your niche. Use keywords, headlines, images, videos, links, or any other elements that can optimize your content for SEO (search engine optimization) and user experience.

8. Drive traffic to your content through SEO (search engine optimization), social media marketing, email marketing, paid advertising, or any other method. This will help you reach more potential customers, generate more leads, and increase your sales.

9. Monetize your content with various methods that suit your goals and preferences. This will help you generate passive income from multiple sources, such as advertising, sponsored posts, affiliate marketing, online courses, e-books, software as a service (SaaS), mobile apps, e-commerce, dropshipping, or any other method.

10. Keep learning and improving your skills, knowledge, and strategies by following the best practices, tips, and trends in blogging.

Blogging is one of the best passive income streams for 2023 and beyond because it is:

- Proven and tested by successful passive income earners who make thousands or millions of dollars per month from blogging.

- Easy and affordable to start with minimal investment, time, or skills. You just need a website or platform where you can publish your content.

- Flexible and adaptable to changing market conditions, customer preferences, or industry standards. You can choose from a wide range of niches, markets, or topics. You can also switch or add niches, markets, or topics as you wish.

- Scalable and profitable to generate high returns, low costs, and high margins. You can earn passive income from multiple sources, multiple platforms, and multiple audiences. You can also earn recurring income from subscription-based products or services.

- Sustainable and consistent to provide long-term value, growth, and stability. You can build a loyal and engaged audience that trusts you and buys from you repeatedly. You can also leverage the power of SEO (search engine optimization), social media marketing, email marketing, paid advertising, or any other method to drive traffic to your content.

If you want to learn more about blogging, you can check out these resources:

- How to Start a Blog That Generates $3817 a Month by Neil Patel

- How to Make Money Blogging (Free Guide for 2023) by Adam Enfroy
- The Ultimate Guide to Making Money Blogging by Ryan Robinson

Podcasting

Podcasting is another popular and lucrative passive income idea. Podcasting is the process of creating and distributing audio content on a website or platform that covers a specific topic or niche. Podcasting is a great way to share your knowledge, passion, or expertise with your audience. Podcasting is also a great way to generate passive income from various sources such as advertising, sponsored episodes, affiliate marketing, online courses, e-books, software as a service (SaaS), mobile apps, e-commerce, dropshipping, or any other method.

How does podcasting work?

Podcasting works in four simple steps:

1. You choose a niche that you are interested in, passionate about, or knowledgeable about.

2. You create a website or platform where you can host and distribute your podcast.

3. You record valuable audio content that attracts your target audience and provides solutions to their problems or needs.

4. You monetize your podcast with various methods that suit your goals and preferences.

How do you start podcasting?

To start podcasting, you need to:

1. Choose a niche that has a large and engaged audience, high demand and low competition, and profitable monetization potential.

2. Choose a name and a logo for your podcast that are catchy, memorable, and relevant to your niche.

3. Choose a podcast hosting service that is reliable, fast, and affordable.

4. Choose a podcasting platform that is easy to use, flexible, and customizable. WordPress is the most popular and recommended podcasting platform because it offers thousands of themes and plugins that can suit any niche or need.

5. Choose a microphone and a software that can help you record and edit your audio content with high quality and clarity.

6. Create valuable audio content that attracts your target audience and provides solutions to their problems or needs. Use keywords, headlines, images, links, or any other elements that can optimize your content for SEO (search engine optimization) and user experience.

7. Drive traffic to your podcast through SEO (search engine optimization), social media marketing, email marketing, paid advertising, or any other method.

How do you succeed with podcasting?

To succeed with podcasting, you need to:

1. Choose a niche that you are interested in, passionate about, or knowledgeable about. This will help you create content that is authentic, engaging, and consistent.

2. Choose a name and a logo for your podcast that are catchy, memorable, and relevant to your niche. This will help you build your brand identity and recognition.

3. Choose a podcast hosting service that is reliable, fast, and affordable. This will help you ensure the security and performance of your podcast.

4. Choose a podcasting platform that is easy to use, flexible, and customizable. WordPress is the most popular and recommended podcasting platform because it offers thousands of themes and plugins that can suit any niche or need.

5. Choose a microphone and a software that can help you record and edit your audio content with high quality and clarity. This will help you create a professional-sounding podcast that can attract and retain your listeners.

6. Create valuable audio content that attracts your target audience and provides solutions to their problems or needs. This will help you establish your authority, credibility, and trustworthiness in your niche. Use keywords, headlines, images, links, or any other elements that can optimize your content for SEO (search engine optimization) and user experience.

7. Drive traffic to your podcast through SEO (search engine optimization), social media marketing, email marketing, paid advertising, or any other method. This will help you reach more potential customers, generate more leads, and increase your sales.

8. Monetize your podcast with various methods that suit your goals and preferences. This will help you generate passive income from multiple sources, such as advertising, sponsored episodes, affiliate marketing, online courses, e-books, software as a service (SaaS), mobile apps, e-commerce, dropshipping, or any other method.

9. Keep learning and improving your skills, knowledge, and strategies by following the best practices, tips, and trends in podcasting.

Podcasting is one of the best passive income streams for 2023 and beyond because it is:

- Proven and tested by successful passive income earners who make thousands or millions of dollars per month from podcasting.

- Easy and affordable to start with minimal investment, time, or skills. You just need a website or platform where you can host and distribute your podcast.

- Flexible and adaptable to changing market conditions, customer preferences, or industry standards. You can choose from a wide range of niches, markets, or topics. You can also switch or add niches, markets, or topics as you wish.

- Scalable and profitable to generate high returns, low costs, and high margins. You can earn passive income from multiple sources, multiple platforms, and multiple audiences. You can also earn recurring income from subscription-based products or services.

- Sustainable and consistent to provide long-term value, growth, and stability. You can build a loyal and engaged audience that trusts you and listens to you repeatedly. You can also leverage the power of SEO (search engine optimization), social media marketing, email marketing, paid advertising, or any other method to drive traffic to your podcast.

If you want to learn more about podcasting, you can check out these resources:

- How to Start a Podcast: Every Single Step for 2023 by Pat Flynn

- How to Start a Podcast in 2023: The Complete Podcasting Tutorial by Adam Enfroy
- The Ultimate Guide to Podcasting by Neil Patel

This concludes chapter 2 of "How to Wake Up Richer Every Day: The Secrets of Making Money While You Sleep". I hope you found it helpful and informative.

CHAPTER
3

How to Set Up Your Own Online Business in Less Than an Hour

You might be wondering how you can start making money online while you sleep. You might think that it's too complicated, too expensive, or too risky to create your own online business. But the truth is, you can set up your own online business in less than an hour, with little or no upfront cost, and start earning passive income from day one.

In this chapter, I will show you how to do it step by step. You don't need any technical skills, any previous experience, or any special equipment. All you need is a computer, an internet connection, and a willingness to learn.

Step 1: Choose a Niche

The first step to creating your own online business is to choose a niche. A niche is a specific topic or area of interest that you want to focus on. For example, some popular niches are health and fitness, personal finance, travel, gaming, fashion, etc.

Choosing a niche is important because it helps you to target a specific audience who are interested in what you have to offer. It also helps you to stand out from the competition and establish yourself as an authority in your field.

To choose a niche, you need to consider three factors:

- **Your passion:** You should choose a niche that you are passionate about or have some knowledge of. This will make it easier for you to create content and products that your audience will love and trust.

- **Your profitability:** You should choose a niche that has enough demand and potential customers who are willing to pay for your products or services. You can use tools like [Google Trends] or [Amazon Best Sellers] to see what topics are popular and trending online.

- **Your competition:** You should choose a niche that is not too saturated or dominated by big brands. You want to find a niche that has some competition, but not too much. You can use tools like [SEMrush] or [Ahrefs] to see how competitive a niche is and what keywords are ranking for it.

Once you have chosen a niche, you need to narrow it down further by defining your target audience. Your target audience is the specific group of people who are most likely to buy your products or services. You need to know who they are, what they want, what they need, what they struggle with, and how you can help them.

To define your target audience, you can use tools like [Facebook Audience Network] or [SurveyMonkey] to create surveys and quizzes that will help you collect data and feedback from your potential customers. You can also use tools like [Quora] or [Reddit] to see what questions and problems your audience has and what solutions they are looking for.

Step 2: Choose a Business Model

The next step to creating your own online business is to choose a business model. A business model is the way you make money from your online business. There are many different types of online business models, but here are some of the most common ones:

- **Affiliate marketing:** Affiliate marketing is when you promote other people's products or services and earn a commission for every sale or action that you generate. You don't need to create your own products or handle any customer service or delivery. You just need to find relevant products or services that match your niche and audience and promote them on your website, blog, social media, email list, etc. Some popular affiliate networks that you can join are [Amazon Associates], [ClickBank], [ShareASale], etc.

- **E-commerce:** E-commerce is when you sell physical or digital products online. You can either create your own products or source them from suppliers or manufacturers. You can also use dropshipping, which is when you sell products without having to stock or ship them yourself. You just need to find reliable suppliers who will handle the inventory and delivery for you. Some popular platforms that you can use to create your own e-commerce store are [Shopify], [WooCommerce], [BigCommerce], etc.

- **Blogging:** Blogging is when you create and publish content on your website or blog that attracts and engages your audience. You can monetize your blog by displaying ads, selling sponsored posts, offering paid memberships, creating online courses, etc. Some popular platforms that you can use to start your own blog are [WordPress], [Medium], [Blogger], etc.

- **Podcasting:** Podcasting is when you create and distribute audio content that entertains or educates your audience. You can monetize your podcast by selling sponsorships, offering paid subscriptions, creating merchandise, etc. Some popular platforms that you can use to start your own podcast are [Anchor], [Spotify], [SoundCloud], etc.

- **YouTube:** YouTube is when you create and upload video content that showcases your skills, talents, hobbies, opinions, etc. You can monetize your YouTube channel by displaying ads, selling merchandise, offering paid memberships, creating online courses, etc. Some popular tools that you can use to create and edit your videos are [Camtasia], [Filmora], [InVideo], etc.

These are just some of the online business models that you can choose from. You can also combine different models or create your own unique one. The key is to choose a business model that suits your niche, audience, skills, and goals.

Step 3: Choose a Platform

The final step to creating your own online business is to choose a platform. A platform is the tool or service that you use to create and manage your online presence. Depending on your business model, you might need one or more platforms to run your online business.

For example, if you choose affiliate marketing as your business model, you might need a website or blog to promote your affiliate products or services. If you choose e-commerce as your business model, you might need an e-commerce store to sell your products online. If you choose podcasting as your business model, you might need a podcast hosting service to distribute your audio content.

There are many different platforms that you can use to create and run your online business. Some of them are free, some of them are paid, and some of them offer both free and paid plans. You need to compare the features, benefits, costs, and limitations of each platform and choose the one that best fits your needs and budget.

Here are some of the most popular platforms that you can use for different online business models:

- Affiliate marketing: WordPress, Medium, Blogger, Wix, Squarespace, etc.
- E-commerce: Shopify, WooCommerce, BigCommerce, Etsy, eBay, etc.
- Blogging: WordPress, Medium, Blogger, Wix, Squarespace, etc.
- Podcasting: Anchor, Spotify, SoundCloud, Podbean, Buzzsprout, etc.

- YouTube: YouTube.

To choose a platform, you need to consider four factors:

- Your ease of use: You should choose a platform that is easy to use and navigate. You don't want to waste time and energy on learning how to use a complicated platform that frustrates you. You want to focus on creating and delivering value to your audience.
- Your customization: You should choose a platform that allows you to customize and personalize your online presence. You want to create a unique and memorable brand identity that reflects your niche, audience, and personality.
- Your scalability: You should choose a platform that can grow with your online business. You want to be able to add more features, functions, products, services, etc. as your online business expands and evolves.
- Your support: You should choose a platform that provides reliable and responsive support. You want to be able to get help and guidance whenever you encounter any issues or challenges with your online business.

Once you have chosen a platform, you need to register an account and set up your online presence. You need to create a domain name, a logo, a tagline, a bio, a contact page, etc. You also need to optimize your online presence for search engines and social media by using keywords, tags, descriptions, images, videos, etc.

Congratulations! You have just learned how to set up your own online business in less than an hour. You have chosen a niche, a business model, and a platform that suit your needs and goals. You have also created and optimized your online presence that attracts and converts your audience.

Now you are ready to start making money online while you sleep. All you need to do is to create valuable content and products that solve your audience's problems and fulfill their desires. You also need to promote your online business by using various marketing strategies such as email marketing, social media marketing, influencer marketing, etc.

Remember that creating an online business is not a one-time event but an ongoing process. You need to constantly test, tweak, and improve your online business based on the feedback and data that you collect from your audience and the market. You also need to keep learning new skills and strategies that will help you grow and scale your online business.

CHAPTER
4

How to Create and Sell Digital Products that Sell Themselves

One of the best ways to make money online while you sleep is to create and sell digital products. Digital products are products that are delivered electronically, such as ebooks, courses, software, apps, etc. They have many advantages over physical products, such as:

- They are easy and cheap to create and distribute. You don't need to invest in inventory, manufacturing, packaging, shipping, etc. You just need to create your digital product once and sell it unlimited times.
- They are scalable and profitable. You don't need to worry about running out of stock or fulfilling orders. You can sell your digital product to as many customers as you want and keep most of the profits for yourself.
- They are passive and recurring. You don't need to spend time and energy on delivering your digital product or providing customer service. You can automate the delivery process and

generate passive income from your digital product for a long time.

But how do you create and sell digital products that sell themselves? How do you create digital products that people want to buy and that stand out from the competition? How do you market and sell your digital products without being pushy or spammy?

In this chapter, I will show you how to do it step by step. You will learn how to:

- Choose a profitable digital product idea that matches your niche and audience
- Create a high-quality digital product that delivers value and solves problems
- Launch and sell your digital product using effective marketing strategies

Step 1: Choose a Profitable Digital Product Idea

The first step to creating and selling digital products is to choose a profitable digital product idea. A profitable digital product idea is one that:

- Has enough demand and potential customers who are willing to pay for it

- Solves a specific problem or fulfills a specific desire for your target audience
- Is unique and different from other existing digital products in your niche

To choose a profitable digital product idea, you need to do some research and validation. You need to find out what your target audience wants, needs, struggles with, and is willing to pay for. You also need to find out what your competitors are offering, what their strengths and weaknesses are, and how you can differentiate yourself from them.

There are many ways to do research and validation for your digital product idea, such as:
- Surveying your existing audience or customers using tools like SurveyMonkey or Google Forms
- Asking questions or conducting interviews with your potential customers using tools like Typeform or Calendly
- Creating landing pages or opt-in forms for your digital product idea using tools like Leadpages or Mailchimp
- Testing your digital product idea with paid ads or organic traffic using tools like Facebook Ads or Google Ads

- Creating minimum viable products MVPs or prototypes for your digital product idea using tools like Gumroad or Teachable

The goal of doing research and validation is to find out if there is enough demand, interest, and feedback for your digital product idea before you invest too much time and money into creating it. You want to make sure that you are creating something that people actually want and are willing to pay for.

Step 2: Create a High-Quality Digital Product

The second step to creating and selling digital products is to create a high-quality digital product. A high-quality digital product is one that:

- Delivers value and solves problems for your target audience
- Is easy to use and understand for your target audience
- Is attractive and professional in design and presentation
- Is consistent and reliable in performance and delivery

To create a high-quality digital product, you need to follow some best practices, such as:

- Planning your digital product content and structure using tools like MindMeister or Trello

- Writing your digital product content using tools like Grammarly or Hemingway
- Designing your digital product graphics using tools like Canva or Adobe Photoshop
- Recording your digital product audio or video using tools like Audacity or Camtasia
- Editing your digital product audio or video using tools like Audacity or Filmora
- Formatting your digital product files using tools like Calibre or HandBrake
- Hosting your digital product files using tools like [Dropbox] or Google Drive

The goal of creating a high-quality digital product is to provide value and satisfaction to your customers. You want to create something that they will love, use, recommend, and buy again.

Step 3: Launch and Sell Your Digital Product

The final step to creating and selling digital products is to launch and sell your digital product. Launching and selling your digital product is the process of getting your digital product in front of your target audience and convincing them to buy it.

To launch and sell your digital product, you need to use effective marketing strategies, such as:

- Creating a sales page or a landing page for your digital product using tools like Leadpages or ClickFunnels
- Writing a sales copy or a landing page copy for your digital product using tools like Copy.ai or Conversion.ai
- Creating a sales video or a landing page video for your digital product using tools like InVideo or Lumen5
- Creating a lead magnet or a freebie for your digital product using tools like Canva or Beacon
- Building an email list or a subscriber list for your digital product using tools like Mailchimp or ConvertKit
- Sending email sequences or newsletters for your digital product using tools like Mailchimp or ConvertKit
- Creating a launch plan or a launch calendar for your digital product using tools like Asana or Google Calendar
- Promoting your digital product on social media platforms using tools like Buffer or Hootsuite
- Promoting your digital product on blogs, podcasts, YouTube channels, etc. using tools like BuzzSumo or PodcastGuests
- Promoting your digital product with paid ads using tools like Facebook Ads or Google Ads

The goal of launching and selling your digital product is to generate traffic, leads, and sales for your digital product. You want to create awareness, interest, and desire for your digital product and persuade your audience to take action and buy it.

In conclusion, you have just learned how to create and sell digital products that sell themselves. You have learned how to:

- Choose a profitable digital product idea that matches your niche and audience
- Create a high-quality digital product that delivers value and solves problems
- Launch and sell your digital product using effective marketing strategies

Now you are ready to start creating and selling your own digital products and make money online while you sleep. All you need to do is to follow the steps and use the tools that I have shared with you in this chapter.

CHAPTER
5

How to Leverage Affiliate Marketing and Earn Commissions on Autopilot

One of the easiest and fastest ways to make money online while you sleep is to leverage affiliate marketing. Affiliate marketing is when you promote other people's products or services and earn a commission for every sale or action that you generate. You don't need to create your own products or handle any customer service or delivery. You just need to find relevant products or services that match your niche and audience and promote them on your website, blog, social media, email list, etc.

Affiliate marketing has many benefits, such as:

- It is low-risk and low-cost. You don't need to invest in inventory, manufacturing, packaging, shipping, etc. You just need to sign up for an affiliate program and get your unique affiliate link.
- It is flexible and diverse. You can choose from a wide range of products or services to promote, from physical goods to digital products, from software to courses, from books to games, etc.

- It is passive and scalable. You don't need to spend time and energy on delivering the products or services or providing customer service. You can automate the promotion process and generate passive income from your affiliate links for a long time.

But how do you leverage affiliate marketing and earn commissions on autopilot? How do you find and join the best affiliate programs for your niche and audience? How do you promote your affiliate links without being annoying or spammy?

In this chapter, I will show you how to do it step by step. You will learn how to:

- Find and join the best affiliate programs for your niche and audience
- Create and optimize your website or blog for affiliate marketing
- Promote your affiliate links using effective marketing strategies

Step 1: Find and Join the Best Affiliate Programs

The first step to leveraging affiliate marketing is to find and join the best affiliate programs for your niche and audience. An affiliate program is a program that allows you to promote a product or service and earn a commission for every sale or action that you generate. There are many different types of affiliate programs, but here are some of the most common ones:

- Pay per sale: Pay per sale is when you earn a percentage of the sale price for every sale that you generate. For example, if you promote a product that costs $100 and has a 10% commission rate, you will earn $10 for every sale that you generate.

- Pay per lead: Pay per lead is when you earn a fixed amount for every lead that you generate. A lead is a potential customer who signs up for a free trial, downloads a free ebook, fills out a form, etc. For example, if you promote a service that pays $5 per lead, you will earn $5 for every lead that you generate.

- Pay per click: Pay per click is when you earn a fixed amount for every click that you generate. A click is when someone clicks on your affiliate link and visits the merchant's website. For example, if you promote a product that pays $0.10 per click, you will earn $0.10 for every click that you generate.

To find and join the best affiliate programs for your niche and audience, you need to consider four factors:

- Your relevance: You should choose affiliate programs that are relevant to your niche and audience. You want to promote products or services that match your content and provide value to your audience.

- Your commission: You should choose affiliate programs that offer high commission rates and generous payment terms. You want to earn as much as possible from your promotions and get paid on time.

- Your support: You should choose affiliate programs that provide reliable and responsive support. You want to be able to get help and guidance whenever you encounter any issues or challenges with your promotions.

- Your reputation: You should choose affiliate programs that have good reputation and credibility. You want to promote products or services that are high-quality, trustworthy, and ethical.

There are many ways to find and join affiliate programs, such as:
- Searching on Google using keywords like "[your niche] + affiliate program" or "[product name] + affiliate program"
- Browsing on affiliate networks like [Amazon Associates], [ClickBank], [ShareASale], etc.
- Asking on forums or groups like [Reddit], [Facebook], [Quora], etc.
- Following influencers or experts in your niche who are already doing affiliate marketing
- Checking out competitors' websites or blogs who are already doing affiliate marketing

Once you have found some potential affiliate programs, you need to apply for them and get approved. You need to fill out an application form with some basic information about yourself and your website or blog. You also need to agree to their terms and conditions and follow their rules and guidelines.

Once you have been approved, you will get access to your unique affiliate link and other promotional materials like banners, images, videos, etc. You will also get access to your dashboard where you can track your performance and earnings.

Step 2: Create and Optimize Your Website or Blog

The second step to leveraging affiliate marketing is to create and optimize your website or blog. A website or blog is your online platform where you can create and publish content that attracts and engages your audience. You can also use your website or blog to promote your affiliate links and generate commissions.

To create and optimize your website or blog, you need to follow some best practices, such as:

- Choosing a domain name that is relevant, memorable, and easy to spell and pronounce
- Choosing a web hosting service that is reliable, fast, and secure

- Choosing a content management system (CMS) that is easy to use and customize
- Choosing a theme or a template that is attractive, professional, and responsive
- Choosing a niche that is specific, profitable, and passionate
- Creating a logo, a tagline, a bio, a contact page, etc. that represent your brand identity and personality
- Creating valuable content that provides information, education, entertainment, or inspiration to your audience
- Optimizing your content for search engines and social media by using keywords, tags, descriptions, images, videos, etc.
- Adding your affiliate links to your content in a natural and ethical way by using anchor texts, call to actions, disclosures, etc.
- Building an email list or a subscriber list by offering a lead magnet or a freebie in exchange for an email address
- Sending email newsletters or sequences that provide value and promote your affiliate links

The goal of creating and optimizing your website or blog is to build trust and authority with your audience. You want to create a loyal and engaged fan base that will visit your website or blog regularly, consume your content, click on your affiliate links, and buy the products or services that you recommend.

Step 3: Promote Your Affiliate Links

The final step to leveraging affiliate marketing is to promote your affiliate links. Promoting your affiliate links is the process of getting more traffic, clicks, and conversions for your affiliate links. You want to reach more people who are interested in your niche and the products or services that you promote.

To promote your affiliate links, you need to use effective marketing strategies, such as:

- Creating more content that is relevant, useful, and engaging for your audience
- Updating and repurposing your existing content to make it fresh and appealing for your audience
- Sharing your content on social media platforms like Facebook, Twitter, Instagram, etc.
- Collaborating with other influencers or experts in your niche who have large and loyal audiences
- Guest posting on other websites or blogs that have high traffic and authority in your niche
- Commenting on other websites or blogs that have high engagement and relevance in your niche
- Participating in forums or groups that have active and interested members in your niche

- Creating videos or podcasts that showcase your skills, talents, hobbies, opinions, etc. related to your niche
- Creating online courses or webinars that teach or demonstrate something valuable related to your niche
- Creating giveaways or contests that offer something attractive related to your niche
- Creating paid ads on platforms like [Facebook Ads] or [Google Ads] that target specific keywords or audiences related to your niche

The goal of promoting your affiliate links is to generate more exposure, interest, and desire for the products or services that you promote. You want to persuade more people to click on your affiliate links and buy the products or services that you recommend.

You have just learned how to leverage affiliate marketing and earn commissions on autopilot. You have learned how to:
- Find and join the best affiliate programs for your niche and audience
- Create and optimize your website or blog for affiliate marketing
- Promote your affiliate links using effective marketing strategies

Now you are ready to start leveraging affiliate marketing and make money online while you sleep. All you need to do is to follow the steps and use the tools that I have shared with you in this chapter.

CHAPTER
6

How to Invest in Stocks, Cryptocurrencies, and Real Estate with Minimal Risk and Maximum Return

One of the smartest and most powerful ways to make money online while you sleep is to invest in stocks, cryptocurrencies, and real estate. Investing is when you put your money into an asset that has the potential to increase in value over time and generate income for you. You can earn money from investing in two ways:

- Capital gains: Capital gains are when you sell your asset for a higher price than you bought it. For example, if you buy a stock for $10 and sell it for $15, you will earn a capital gain of $5.

- Dividends or interest: Dividends or interest are when you receive a regular payment from your asset for holding it. For example, if you own a stock that pays a dividend of $0.50 per share every quarter, you will receive $0.50 for every share that you own every three months.

Investing has many benefits, such as:

- It is passive and recurring. You don't need to spend time and energy on creating or delivering a product or service. You just need to buy and hold your asset and let it grow and pay you over time.

- It is scalable and profitable. You don't need to worry about running out of inventory or fulfilling orders. You can invest as much as you want and earn as much as you want from your asset.

- It is diversified and flexible. You can choose from a wide range of assets to invest in, from stocks to cryptocurrencies, from real estate to commodities, etc. You can also adjust your portfolio according to your risk tolerance, time horizon, and goals.

But how do you invest in stocks, cryptocurrencies, and real estate with minimal risk and maximum return? How do you find and buy the best assets for your niche and audience? How do you manage and grow your portfolio without being overwhelmed or stressed?

In this chapter, I will show you how to do it step by step. You will learn how to:

- Find and buy the best stocks for your niche and audience

- Find and buy the best cryptocurrencies for your niche and audience
- Find and buy the best real estate for your niche and audience

Step 1: Find and Buy the Best Stocks

The first step to investing online while you sleep is to find and buy the best stocks for your niche and audience. A stock is a share of ownership in a company that trades on a stock exchange. You can buy and sell stocks through an online broker or a trading platform.

To find and buy the best stocks, you need to consider four factors:

- Your niche: You should choose stocks that are relevant to your niche and audience. You want to invest in companies that match your content and provide value to your audience.
- Your performance: You should choose stocks that have strong financial performance and growth potential. You want to invest in companies that have high earnings, revenue, cash flow, etc.
- Your valuation: You should choose stocks that are undervalued or fairly valued. You want to invest in companies that have low price-to-earnings (P/E), price-to-book (P/B), price-to-sales (P/S), etc.
- Your dividend: You should choose stocks that pay regular and high dividends. You want to invest in companies that have

high dividend yield, dividend growth, dividend payout ratio, etc.

There are many ways to find and buy stocks, such as:
- Searching on Google using keywords like "[your niche] + best stocks" or "[your niche] + dividend stocks"
- Browsing on stock screeners like [Finviz] or [Yahoo Finance] to filter stocks by various criteria
- Following analysts or experts who provide stock recommendations or ratings
- Reading financial news or reports that cover the latest trends and developments in the stock market
- Checking out competitors' websites or blogs who are already investing in stocks

Once you have found some potential stocks, you need to do some research and analysis. You need to check their financial statements, earnings reports, analyst opinions, etc. You also need to compare their performance, valuation, dividend, etc. with their peers and the market.

Once you have done your research and analysis, you need to decide how much to invest in each stock. You need to consider your budget, risk tolerance, diversification, etc. You also need to decide when to buy and sell each stock. You need to consider your entry point, exit point, stop loss, etc.

Step 2: Find and Buy the Best Cryptocurrencies

The second step to investing online while you sleep is to find and buy the best cryptocurrencies for your niche and audience. A cryptocurrency is a digital currency that uses cryptography to secure its transactions and control its creation. You can buy and sell cryptocurrencies through an online exchange or a wallet.

To find and buy the best cryptocurrencies, you need to consider four factors:

- Your niche: You should choose cryptocurrencies that are relevant to your niche and audience. You want to invest in cryptocurrencies that match your content and provide value to your audience.
- Your innovation: You should choose cryptocurrencies that have innovative features and functions. You want to invest in cryptocurrencies that have unique and advanced technology, such as smart contracts, decentralized applications, etc.
- Your adoption: You should choose cryptocurrencies that have high adoption and usage. You want to invest in cryptocurrencies that have large and active communities, partnerships, integrations, etc.

- Your volatility: You should choose cryptocurrencies that have low volatility and high stability. You want to invest in cryptocurrencies that have low price fluctuations, high liquidity, etc.

There are many ways to find and buy cryptocurrencies, such as:
- Searching on Google using keywords like "[your niche] + best cryptocurrencies" or "[your niche] + stablecoins"
- Browsing on cryptocurrency trackers like [CoinMarketCap] or [CoinGecko] to filter cryptocurrencies by various criteria
- Following influencers or experts who provide cryptocurrency recommendations or ratings
- Reading cryptocurrency news or reports that cover the latest trends and developments in the cryptocurrency market
- Checking out competitors' websites or blogs who are already investing in cryptocurrencies

Once you have found some potential cryptocurrencies, you need to do some research and analysis. You need to check their whitepapers, roadmaps, team members, etc. You also need to compare their innovation, adoption, volatility, etc. with their peers and the market.

Once you have done your research and analysis, you need to decide how much to invest in each cryptocurrency. You need to consider your budget, risk tolerance, diversification, etc. You also need to decide when to buy and sell each cryptocurrency. You need to consider your entry point, exit point, stop loss, etc.

Step 3: Find and Buy the Best Real Estate

The third step to investing online while you sleep is to find and buy the best real estate for your niche and audience. Real estate is property that consists of land and buildings. You can buy and sell real estate through an online platform or a broker.

To find and buy the best real estate, you need to consider four factors:

- Your niche: You should choose real estate that is relevant to your niche and audience. You want to invest in real estate that matches your content and provides value to your audience.
- Your location: You should choose real estate that is located in a desirable and profitable area. You want to invest in real estate that has high demand, low supply, high appreciation, etc.
- Your income: You should choose real estate that generates regular and high income for you. You want to invest in real estate that has high rental yield, occupancy rate, cash flow, etc.

- Your expense: You should choose real estate that has low expense and maintenance for you. You want to invest in real estate that has low taxes, fees, repairs, etc.

There are many ways to find and buy real estate, such as:
- Searching on Google using keywords like "[your niche] + best real estate" or "[your niche] + rental properties"
- Browsing on real estate platforms like [Zillow] or [Trulia] to filter real estate by various criteria
- Following agents or experts who provide real estate recommendations or ratings
- Reading real estate news or reports that cover the latest trends and developments in the real estate market
- Checking out competitors' websites or blogs who are already investing in real estate

Once you have found some potential real estate, you need to do some research and analysis. You need to check their features, amenities, photos, reviews, etc. You also need to compare their location, income, expense, etc. with their peers and the market.

Once you have done your research and analysis, you need to decide how much to invest in each real estate. You need to consider your budget, risk tolerance, diversification, etc. You also need to decide when to buy and sell each real estate. You need to consider your entry point, exit point, stop loss, etc.

You have just learned how to invest in stocks, cryptocurrencies, and real estate with minimal risk and maximum return. You have learned how to:

- Find and buy the best stocks for your niche and audience
- Find and buy the best cryptocurrencies for your niche and audience
- Find and buy the best real estate for your niche and audience

Now you are ready to start investing online while you sleep and make money from capital gains and dividends or interest. All you need to do is to follow the steps and use the tools that I have shared with you in this chapter.

CHAPTER
7

How to Outsource and Automate Your Business Operations

One of the most powerful ways to make money while you sleep is to outsource and automate your business operations. Outsourcing and automation can help you save time, money, and energy, while increasing your productivity, quality, and profitability. In this chapter, we will explore how to outsource and automate your business operations, and what benefits you can expect from doing so.

Outsourcing is the process of hiring external parties to perform tasks or services that are not part of your core competencies or that you don't want to do yourself. Automation is the use of technology or software to perform tasks or processes without human intervention. Both outsourcing and automation can help you leverage your strengths, delegate your weaknesses, and focus on your most important goals.

Outsourcing and automation can benefit your business in many ways, such as:

- Reducing costs: Outsourcing and automation can help you lower your labor costs, overhead expenses, and operational inefficiencies. For example, you can outsource tasks such as accounting, marketing, customer service, or web development to freelancers or agencies that charge lower rates than hiring full-time employees. You can also automate tasks such as invoicing, email marketing, social media posting, or data entry using software tools that require minimal or no human input.

- Increasing quality: Outsourcing and automation can help you improve the quality of your products or services by hiring experts or using reliable systems that can deliver better results than doing it yourself. For example, you can outsource tasks such as graphic design, copywriting, editing, or proofreading to professionals who have the skills and experience to create high-quality content. You can also automate tasks such as testing, debugging, or quality assurance using software tools that can detect and fix errors more efficiently than manual methods.

- Scaling up: Outsourcing and automation can help you grow your business faster and easier by allowing you to handle more work or customers without increasing your workload or stress. For example, you can outsource tasks such as lead generation, sales, or fulfillment to partners or platforms that can help you reach more potential or existing customers. You can also automate tasks such as scheduling, follow-up, or feedback using software tools that can help you manage your relationships with your customers more effectively.

- Freeing up time: Outsourcing and automation can help you save time and energy by eliminating or reducing the amount of work or tasks that you have to do yourself. This can give you more freedom and flexibility to pursue other opportunities or activities that are more valuable or enjoyable for you. For example, you can outsource tasks such as research, analysis, or reporting to assistants or consultants who can provide you with the information or insights that you need. You can also automate tasks such as backup, security, or maintenance using software tools that can protect and optimize your systems without requiring your attention.

To outsource and automate your business operations successfully, you need to follow some best practices, such as:

- Identify what to outsource and automate: The first step is to analyze your business processes and identify which tasks or services are suitable for outsourcing or automation. You should consider factors such as the complexity, frequency, cost, value, and impact of each task or service on your business goals. Generally speaking, you should outsource or automate tasks or services that are repetitive, low-value, time-consuming, non-essential, or outside your expertise.

- Choose the right providers or tools: The second step is to find and select the best external parties or software solutions that can perform the tasks or services that you want to outsource or automate. You should consider factors such as the quality, reliability, price, reputation, compatibility, and support of each provider or tool. You should also do some research and comparison before making a decision. You can use online platforms such as Upwork, Fiverr, Zapier, IFTTT, etc., to find and hire freelancers, agencies, or software tools for various outsourcing or automation needs.

- Communicate clearly and effectively: The third step is to communicate clearly and effectively with your providers or tools about the expectations and requirements of the tasks or services that you want them to perform. You should provide them with detailed instructions, specifications, deadlines, feedbacks, etc., to ensure that they understand what you want and how you want it done. You should also monitor their progress and performance regularly and address any issues or problems promptly.

- Evaluate the results and outcomes: The fourth step is to evaluate the results and outcomes of the tasks or services that you have outsourced or automated. You should measure the benefits and costs of outsourcing or automation in terms of time saved, money saved, quality improved, revenue increased, customer satisfaction enhanced etc., compared to doing it yourself. You should also review the feedbacks from your customers, partners etc., regarding the quality of your products or services delivered by outsourcing or automation. Based on the evaluation results ,you should make adjustments or improvements as needed.

Outsourcing and automation are powerful strategies that can help you make money while you sleep by optimizing your business operations. By outsourcing and automating the right tasks or services, you can reduce costs, increase quality, scale up, and free up time for your business. However, you need to be careful and strategic when outsourcing or automating your business operations, as there are also some risks and challenges involved, such as losing control, compromising security, facing legal issues etc., that you need to be aware of and manage properly. Therefore, you should always do your due diligence and research before outsourcing or automating your business operations, and follow the best practices mentioned above to ensure a successful outcome.

In this chapter, we have learned how to outsource and automate your business operations, and what benefits you can expect from doing so. However, outsourcing and automation are not without risks and challenges. In this section, we will discuss some of the common pitfalls and problems that you may encounter when outsourcing or automating your business operations, and how to avoid or overcome them.

Some of the common risks and challenges of outsourcing and automation are:

- Losing control: Outsourcing and automation can make you lose some degree of control over your business processes, as you are relying on external parties or software solutions to perform tasks or services for you. This can expose you to potential issues such as miscommunication, misunderstanding, delays, errors, fraud, etc., that can affect the quality or timeliness of your products or services. To avoid or minimize this risk, you should choose reputable and reliable providers or tools that have proven track records and positive reviews. You should also establish clear and frequent communication channels with your providers or tools, and monitor their progress and performance regularly. You should also have contingency plans in case of emergencies or failures.

- Compromising security: Outsourcing and automation can also compromise the security of your business data, information, or systems, as you are sharing or granting access to them with external parties or software solutions. This can expose you to potential threats such as hacking, phishing, malware, identity theft, etc., that can damage or steal your data, information, or systems. To avoid or minimize this risk, you should choose providers or tools that have high standards and certifications for data protection and security. You should also use encryption, passwords, firewalls, etc., to secure your data, information, or systems. You should also limit the access and permissions that you give to your providers or tools, and revoke them when they are no longer needed.

- Facing legal issues: Outsourcing and automation can also expose you to legal issues such as contracts, taxes, regulations, intellectual property rights etc., that can vary depending on the location, industry, or nature of your business. This can expose you to potential disputes, fines, penalties etc., that can affect your reputation or profitability. To avoid or minimize this risk, you should consult with legal experts or advisors before outsourcing or automating your business operations. You should also review and understand the terms and conditions of the contracts or agreements that you sign with your providers or tools. You should also comply with the laws and regulations that apply to your business in different jurisdictions.

Outsourcing and automation are powerful strategies that can help you make money while you sleep by optimizing your business operations. However, they also come with some risks and challenges that you need to be aware of and manage properly. By following the best practices and tips mentioned in this chapter, you can outsource and automate your business operations successfully and safely. In the next chapter, we will explore how to create passive income streams that can generate money for you even when you are not working.

CHAPTER
8

How to Scale and Grow Your Passive Income Empire

In the previous chapters, we have learned how to create and optimize various passive income streams that can generate money for you while you sleep. However, creating passive income streams is not enough. You also need to scale and grow your passive income empire to achieve your financial goals and dreams. In this chapter, we will explore how to scale and grow your passive income empire, and what strategies and tips you can use to do so.

Scaling and growing your passive income empire means increasing the amount of money that you earn from your passive income streams without increasing the amount of work or time that you invest in them. Scaling and growing your passive income empire can benefit you in many ways, such as:

- Increasing your wealth: Scaling and growing your passive income empire can help you increase your wealth by multiplying your income sources and amounts. This can help you achieve financial freedom, security, and abundance faster and easier.

- Increasing your impact: Scaling and growing your passive income empire can also help you increase your impact by reaching more people and providing more value with your products or services. This can help you make a positive difference in the world and fulfill your purpose or mission.

- Increasing your happiness: Scaling and growing your passive income empire can also help you increase your happiness by giving you more freedom, flexibility, and fulfillment. This can help you enjoy your life more and pursue your passions or hobbies.

To scale and grow your passive income empire successfully, you need to follow some best practices, such as:

- **Diversify your portfolio:** The first step is to diversify your portfolio of passive income streams by creating or investing in different types of products or services that can generate passive income for you. You should consider factors such as the market demand, profitability, risk, scalability, etc., of each product or service. Generally speaking, you should diversify your portfolio across different categories such as:

i. Content: Content is any type of information or entertainment that you create or curate and distribute online or offline, such as books, blogs, podcasts, videos, courses, etc. Content can generate passive income for you by monetizing your audience through advertising, sponsorship, subscription, affiliate marketing, etc.

ii. Software: Software is any type of application or program that you create or license and offer online or offline, such as apps, games, websites, plugins, etc. Software can generate passive income for you by monetizing your users through sales, subscription, licensing, etc.

iii. Products: Products are any type of physical or digital goods that you create or source and sell online or offline, such as ebooks, audiobooks, music, art, merchandise, etc. Products can generate passive income for you by monetizing your customers through sales, subscription, dropshipping etc.

iv. Services: Services are any type of professional or personal assistance that you provide or outsource online or offline, such as consulting, coaching, freelancing etc. Services can generate passive income for you by monetizing your clients through recurring fees, commissions etc.

v. Assets: Assets are any type of property or resource that you own or control online or offline that can generate value for you over time such as real estate , stocks , bonds , cryptocurrencies , etc. Assets can generate passive income for you by monetizing their appreciation , dividends , interest , rent etc.

By diversifying your portfolio of passive income streams , you can reduce the risk of losing all your income if one stream fails or declines , and increase the potential of earning more income from multiple streams.

- **Automate your systems:** The second step is to automate your systems of passive income streams by using technology or software to perform tasks or processes without human intervention. You should consider factors such as the complexity , frequency , cost , value , and impact of each task or process on your passive income streams. Generally speaking , you should automate tasks or processes that are repetitive , low-value , time-consuming , non-essential , or outside your expertise.

By automating your systems of passive income streams , you can save time , money , and energy , while increasing productivity , quality , and profitability.

- Delegate your tasks: The third step is to delegate your tasks of passive income streams by hiring external parties to perform tasks or services that are not part of your core competencies or that you don't want to do yourself. You should consider factors such as the quality , reliability , price , reputation , compatibility , and support of each external party. You should also do some research and comparison before making a decision. You can use online platforms such as Upwork, Fiverr, Zapier, IFTTT, etc., to find and hire freelancers , agencies , or software tools for various outsourcing needs.

By delegating your tasks of passive income streams , you can leverage your strengths , delegate your weaknesses , and focus on your most important goals.

- Optimize your performance: The fourth step is to optimize your performance of passive income streams by measuring the benefits and costs of each stream in terms of time invested , money earned , quality delivered , revenue increased , customer satisfaction enhanced etc., compared to your goals and expectations. You should also review the feedbacks from your audience , users , customers , clients etc., regarding the value of your products or services. Based on the performance results , you should make adjustments or improvements as needed.

By optimizing your performance of passive income streams , you can improve the efficiency , effectiveness , and excellence of your products or services.

- **Scale up your reach:** The fifth step is to scale up your reach of passive income streams by increasing the number of people who are aware of , interested in , or engaged with your products or services. You should consider factors such as the market size , demand , competition , trends etc., of each product or service. You should also use various marketing strategies and channels such as SEO, social media, email marketing, influencer marketing, etc., to promote and distribute your products or services.

By scaling up your reach of passive income streams , you can grow your audience , users , customers , clients etc., and generate more income from them.

- Innovate your offerings: The sixth step is to innovate your offerings of passive income streams by creating or investing in new or improved products or services that can generate passive income for you. You should consider factors such as the market needs , gaps , opportunities etc., of each product or service. You should also use various innovation methods and tools such as brainstorming, prototyping, testing, feedback, etc., to develop and launch your products or services.

By innovating your offerings of passive income streams , you can create more value for your audience , users , customers , clients etc., and differentiate yourself from your competitors.

Scaling and growing your passive income empire are essential steps that can help you make money while you sleep by multiplying your income sources and amounts. However, scaling and growing your passive income empire are not easy tasks that require planning, execution, and evaluation. Therefore, you should always follow the best practices and tips mentioned in this chapter to ensure a successful outcome.

CHAPTER
9

How to Manage Your Finances and Taxes as a Passive Income Earner

In the previous chapters, we have learned how to create, optimize, scale, and grow various passive income streams that can generate money for you while you sleep. However, making money is not enough. You also need to manage your finances and taxes as a passive income earner to keep more of what you earn and avoid legal troubles. In this chapter, we will explore how to manage your finances and taxes as a passive income earner, and what strategies and tips you can use to do so.

Managing your finances and taxes as a passive income earner means keeping track of your income and expenses, budgeting and saving your money, investing and growing your wealth, and paying your taxes on time and correctly. Managing your finances and taxes as a passive income earner can benefit you in many ways, such as:

- Increasing your net worth: Managing your finances and taxes as a passive income earner can help you increase your net worth by maximizing your income, minimizing your expenses, and optimizing your investments. This can help you achieve financial independence, security, and abundance faster and easier.

- Reducing your stress: Managing your finances and taxes as a passive income earner can also help you reduce your stress by avoiding or resolving financial problems, such as debt, cash flow, or tax issues. This can help you improve your mental and emotional health and well-being.

- Enhancing your reputation: Managing your finances and taxes as a passive income earner can also help you enhance your reputation by complying with the laws and regulations that apply to your business and income. This can help you avoid legal troubles, penalties, or audits that can damage your credibility or profitability.

To manage your finances and taxes as a passive income earner successfully, you need to follow some best practices, such as:

- Track your income and expenses: The first step is to track your income and expenses from all your passive income streams on a regular basis, such as daily, weekly, monthly, quarterly, or yearly. You should consider factors such as the source, amount, frequency, currency, etc., of each income or expense. You should also use various tools or methods to record and organize your income and expenses, such as spreadsheets, apps, software, etc.

By tracking your income and expenses from all your passive income streams , you can have a clear picture of your financial situation , performance , and progress.

- **Budget and save your money:** The second step is to budget and save your money from all your passive income streams according to your financial goals and needs. You should consider factors such as the percentage , amount , frequency , purpose , etc., of each budget or saving. You should also use various tools or methods to plan and execute your budget or saving , such as envelopes , jars , accounts , etc.

By budgeting and saving your money from all your passive income streams , you can allocate your money wisely , efficiently , and effectively.

- **Invest and grow your wealth:** The third step is to invest and grow your wealth from all your passive income streams by creating or investing in different types of assets that can generate more value for you over time , such as real estate , stocks , bonds , cryptocurrencies , etc. You should consider factors such as the risk , return , liquidity , diversification , etc., of each asset. You should also use various tools or methods to research and manage your investments , such as books , blogs , podcasts , videos , courses , apps , software , etc.

By investing and growing your wealth from all your passive income streams , you can multiply your money faster and easier.

- **Pay your taxes on time and correctly:** The fourth step is to pay your taxes on time and correctly from all your passive income streams according to the laws and regulations that apply to your business and income. You should consider factors such as the type , rate , deadline , deduction , exemption , etc., of each tax. You should also use various tools or methods to calculate and file your taxes , such as calculators , forms , software , etc. You should also consult with tax experts or advisors before paying or filing your taxes.

By paying your taxes on time and correctly from all your passive income streams , you can comply with the law avoid penalties or audits.

Managing your finances and taxes as a passive income earner are crucial steps that can help you make money while you sleep by keeping more of what you earn avoiding legal troubles. However managing finances taxes are not simple tasks that require discipline knowledge.

CHAPTER 10

How to Enjoy Your Life and Achieve Your Goals with Passive Income

Passive income is the money that you earn without actively working for it. It is the opposite of active income, which is the money that you earn by exchanging your time and skills for money. Passive income can come from various sources, such as investments, royalties, online businesses, rental properties, etc.

Passive income can help you enjoy your life and achieve your goals in many ways. Here are some of the benefits of passive income:

- It gives you more freedom and flexibility. With passive income, you don't have to work for a boss, follow a schedule, or commute to an office. You can work when you want, where you want, and how you want. You can also choose to work on the projects that interest you and align with your values. You can travel the world, pursue your hobbies, spend more time with your family and friends, or do whatever makes you happy.

- It reduces your stress and anxiety. With passive income, you don't have to worry about losing your job, getting a pay cut, or meeting deadlines. You don't have to deal with office politics, toxic coworkers, or demanding clients. You don't have to live paycheck to paycheck, struggle to pay your bills, or save for emergencies. You can enjoy a more relaxed and peaceful lifestyle.

- It increases your wealth and security. With passive income, you can earn more money than you spend, which allows you to save and invest more. You can build your net worth, create multiple streams of income, and diversify your portfolio. You can also take advantage of compound interest, tax benefits, and inflation protection. You can achieve financial independence, retire early, or leave a legacy for your loved ones.

- It helps you grow and learn. With passive income, you can challenge yourself to create value for others, solve problems, and innovate. You can also learn new skills, acquire new knowledge, and explore new opportunities. You can expand your network, collaborate with other people, and get feedback from your customers. You can also experiment with different ideas, test different strategies, and improve your results.

How to Create Passive Income

Creating passive income is not easy, but it is possible if you follow these steps:

- Identify your passion and purpose. The first step is to find out what you are passionate about and what purpose you want to serve in the world. This will help you choose a niche that suits your interests, skills, and values. It will also help you stay motivated and focused on your goals.

- Research your market and audience. The second step is to research the market and the audience that you want to serve. This will help you understand their needs, wants, problems, and desires. It will also help you find out what products or services already exist in the market, what gaps or opportunities there are, and what value proposition you can offer.

- Create your product or service. The third step is to create your product or service that provides value to your audience. This can be anything that solves a problem, fulfills a need, satisfies a want, or enhances a desire. It can be a physical product, a digital product, a service, a membership site, a course, a book, etc.

- Launch your product or service. The fourth step is to launch your product or service to the market. This involves setting up your website or platform, creating your sales funnel or process, generating traffic or leads, converting prospects into customers or clients, and delivering your product or service.

- Automate and scale your product or service. The fifth step is to automate and scale your product or service so that it generates passive income for you. This involves outsourcing or delegating tasks that are not essential or enjoyable for you, using tools or systems that streamline or optimize your operations, creating recurring revenue models or passive income streams, and expanding your reach or impact.

Passive income is the key to enjoying your life and achieving your goals with less stress and more freedom. By following the steps above,
you can create passive income from various sources that suit your passion and purpose.
You can wake up richer every day by making money while you sleep.

I hope this chapter has inspired you to take action and start creating passive income today!

CONCLUSION

The Future of Passive Income and How to Stay Ahead of the Curve

You have reached the end of this book, but not the end of your journey. You have learned the secrets of making money while you sleep, and how to create passive income from various sources that suit your passion and purpose. You have also learned how to enjoy your life and achieve your goals with passive income, and how to automate and scale your product or service.

But the world is changing fast, and so is the passive income landscape. New technologies, trends, and opportunities are emerging every day, and you need to be ready to adapt and evolve. Here are some tips on how to stay ahead of the curve and future-proof your passive income:

- Keep learning and growing. Passive income is not a one-time thing, but a continuous process. You need to keep learning new skills, acquiring new knowledge, and exploring new opportunities. You need to keep improving your product or service, testing different strategies, and measuring your results. You need to keep challenging yourself to create more value for others, solve more problems, and innovate more.

- Keep diversifying and expanding. Passive income is not a single source, but a multiple stream. You need to diversify your portfolio, create multiple streams of income, and reduce your risk. You need to expand your reach, impact more people, and increase your revenue. You need to leverage your network, collaborate with others, and get referrals.

- Keep adding value and serving others. Passive income is not a selfish thing, but a generous thing. You need to add value to others, solve their problems, fulfill their needs, satisfy their wants, or enhance their desires. You need to serve others, help them achieve their goals, make them happy, or improve their lives. You need to create a loyal fan base, build trust and credibility, and get positive feedback.

By following these tips, you can stay ahead of the curve and future-proof your passive income. You can wake up richer every day by making money while you sleep.

I hope this book has inspired you to take action and start creating passive income today! Thank you for reading!

ACKNOWLEDGMENT

I would like to express my gratitude to all the people who helped me write this book. Without their support, guidance, and encouragement, this book would not have been possible.

First of all, I would like to thank my editor, Moses Johnson, for his valuable feedback, suggestions, and revisions. He helped me polish my writing, clarify my ideas, and improve my structure. He was always patient, professional, and supportive.

Secondly, I would like to thank my family and friends for their love, understanding, and motivation. They were always there for me, cheering me on, listening to me, and inspiring me. They helped me let go of the past and focus on the future.

Thirdly, I would like to thank my readers for their interest, curiosity, and trust. They are the reason why I wrote this book. I hope this book will help them let go of the past and wake up richer every day by making money while they sleep.

Finally, I would like to thank myself for taking on this challenge and completing this book. It was not easy, but it was worth it. I learned a lot, grew a lot, and achieved a lot. I am proud of myself and happy with the result.

Thank you all!